This
STAMP ALBUM
Belongs to

....

We hope that this Book will be useful and, practical as we wanted to be.

If you think that this Book is good enough, and if it had been useful in any way, please make sure to LEAVE A REVIEW ON AMAZON REVIEW SECTION.

We would definitely love to read your honest opinions, and feedback, it will make us create better products for you in the future

THANK YOU VERY MUCH FOR YOU SUPPORT.

Stamp Album

Country: ....

Notes: ....
....
....

Stamp Album

Country: ....

Notes : ....
....
....

Stamp Album

Country: ....

Notes : ....
....
....

Stamp Album

Country: ....

Notes : ....
....
....

Stamp Album

Country: ....

Notes : ....
....
....

Stamp Album

Country: ....

Notes : ....
....
....

Stamp Album

Country: ....

Notes: ....
....
....

Stamp Album

Country: ....

Notes: ....
....
....

Stamp Album

Country: ....

Notes : ....
....
....

Stamp Album

Country: ....

Notes: ....
....
....

Stamp Album

Country: ....

Notes : ....
....
....

Stamp Album

Country: ....

Notes: ....
....
....

Stamp Album

Country: ....

Notes : ....
....
....

Stamp Album

Country: ....

Notes: ....
....
....

Stamp Album

Country: ....

Notes : ....
....
....

Stamp Album

Country: ....

Notes : ....
....
....

Stamp Album

Country: ....

Notes : ....
....
....

Stamp Album

Country: ....

Notes: ....
....
....

Stamp Album

Country: ....

Notes: ....
....
....

Stamp Album

Country: ....

Notes: ....
....
....

Stamp Album

Country: ....

Notes: ....
....
....

Stamp Album

Country: ....

Notes : ....
....
....

Stamp Album

Country: ....

Notes: ....
....
....

Stamp Album

Country: ....

Notes: ....
....
....

Stamp Album

Country: ....

Notes: ....
....
....

Stamp Album

Country: ....

Notes: ....
....
....

Stamp Album

Country: ....

Notes: ....
....
....

Stamp Album

Country: ....

Notes: ....
....
....

Stamp Album

Country: ....

Notes: ....
....
....

Stamp Album

Country: ....

Notes: ....
....
....

Stamp Album

Country: ....

Notes: ....
....
....

Stamp Album

Country: ....

Notes: ....
....
....

Stamp Album

Country: ....

Notes : ....
....
....

Stamp Album

Country: ....

Notes: ....
....
....

Stamp Album

Country: ....

Notes : ....
....
....

Stamp Album

Country: ....

Notes: ....
....
....

Stamp Album

Country: ....

Notes : ....
....
....

Stamp Album

Country: ....

Notes: ....
....
....

Stamp Album

Country: ....

Notes: ....
....
....

Stamp Album

Country: ....

Notes: ....
....
....

Stamp Album

Country: ....

Notes: ....
....
....

Stamp Album

Country: ....

Notes: ....
....
....

Stamp Album

Country: ....

Notes: ....
....
....

Stamp Album

Country: ....

Notes: ....
....
....

Stamp Album

Country: ....

Notes : ....
....
....

Stamp Album

Country: ....

Notes : ....
....
....

Stamp Album

Country: ....

Notes : ....
....
....

Stamp Album

Country: ....

Notes : ....
....
....

Stamp Album

Country: ....

Notes : ....
....
....

Stamp Album

Country: ....

Notes : ....
....
....

Stamp Album

Country: ....

Notes: ....
....
....

Stamp Album

Country: ....

Notes: ....
....
....

Stamp Album

Country: ....

Notes: ....
....
....

Stamp Album

Country: ....

Notes: ....
....
....

Stamp Album

Country: ....

Notes: ....
....
....

Stamp Album

Country: ....

Notes : ....
....
....

Stamp Album

Country: ....

Notes: ....
....
....

Stamp Album

Country: ....

Notes : ....
....
....

Stamp Album

Country: ....

Notes: ....
....
....

Stamp Album

Country: ....

Notes: ....
....
....

Stamp Album

Country: ....

Notes: ....
....
....

Stamp Album

Country: ....

Notes : ....
....
....

Stamp Album

Country: ....

Notes: ....
....
....

Stamp Album

Country: ....

Notes : ....
....
....

Stamp Album

Country: ....

Notes: ....
....
....

Stamp Album

Country: ....

Notes: ....
....
....

Stamp Album

Country: ....

Notes: ....
....
....

Stamp Album

Country: ....

Notes: ....
....
....

Stamp Album

Country: ....

Notes: ....
....
....

Stamp Album

Country: ....

Notes: ....
....
....

Stamp Album

Country: ....

Notes: ....
....
....

Stamp Album

Country: ....

Notes: ....
....
....

Stamp Album

Country: ....

Notes : ....
....
....

Stamp Album

Country: ....

Notes: ....
....
....

Stamp Album

Country: ....

Notes: ....
....
....

Stamp Album

Country: ....

Notes: ....
....
....

Stamp Album

Country: ....

Notes : ....
....
....

Stamp Album

Country: ....

Notes: ....
....
....

Stamp Album

Country: ....

Notes: ....
....
....

Stamp Album

Country: ....

Notes: ....
....
....

Stamp Album

Country: ....

Notes: ....
....
....

Stamp Album

Country: ....

Notes: ....
....
....

Stamp Album

Country: ....

Notes: ....
....
....

Stamp Album

Country: ....

Notes: ....
....
....

Stamp Album

Country: ....

Notes: ....
....
....

Stamp Album

Country: ....

Notes: ....
....
....

Stamp Album

Country: ....

Notes: ....
....
....

Stamp Album

Country: ....

Notes : ....
....
....

Stamp Album

Country: ....

Notes: ....
....
....

Stamp Album

Country: ....

Notes: ....
....
....

Stamp Album

Country: ....

Notes : ....
....
....

Stamp Album

Country: ....

Notes : ....
....
....

Stamp Album

Country: ....

Notes: ....

....

....

Stamp Album

Country: ....

Notes : ....
....
....

Stamp Album

Country: ....

Notes : ....
....
....

Stamp Album

Country: ....

Notes: ....
....
....

Stamp Album

Country: ....

Notes: ....
....
....

Printed in Dunstable, United Kingdom